The Rescue Plan

Told by Carine Mackenzie
Illustrations by Fred Apps

Published by Christian Focus
Geanies House, Fearn, Tain, Ross-shire, IV20 1TW,
Scotland
© 1999 Christian Focus Publications
Printed in Singapore

Noah was a very good man. He pleased God in the way that he lived. Noah and his wife had three fine sons called Shem, Ham and Japheth.

Other people were not like Noah. They were nasty and violent. They didn't care about God. Their minds were full of bad thoughts all the time. They were so bad that God was sorry that he had made them.

'I will destroy this violent world,' God said.

But God did not want to harm good Noah and his family so he gave him a message.

'Build a big boat,' God told Noah.

'I'm going to send a flood over the earth to destroy all the bad people but I promise to keep you and your family safe inside the big boat.'

Noah believed what God told him and obeyed his instructions.

God gave Noah detailed orders about the building of the big boat (sometimes called ark). Noah carried out every single instruction.

It was a huge task - 140 metres long, 23 metres wide and 14 metres high - made of good wood and painted with tar inside and out to keep it waterproof. There was a roof on top and a door on one side. A space of about half a metre was made between the sides and the roof - this would let fresh air come in.

Noah built a lower, a middle and an upper floor, and rooms for his family to stay.

God also told Noah to take every kind of animal into the ark - two of each sort - a male and a female - to keep them safe from the flood. Enough food to feed them all for a long time had to be taken too.

Noah had to take seven pairs of some animals - those that were needed for food and those used for sacrificing - and seven pairs of each kind of bird.

After many years of hard work the ark was finished. Noah listened to what God said and did everything just as he told him.

Noah and his wife and Shem, Ham and Japheth and their wives all went into the ark. All the animals came in just as God had ordered. God had promised to keep them safe. He had provided this means of escape. When they were all safely inside, God shut the door.

The rain started to fall - down it poured - for days and days. For forty days the rain kept coming down and the floods kept coming up. The ark was lifted up off the ground and floated on top of the water. Just as God had warned, every living thing died - people, animals, birds and reptiles.

Only those with Noah in the ark were safe.

For 150 days the water completely flooded the earth. But God had not forgotten about Noah and the animals in the ark. The wind began to blow and dry up the water. Gradually the flood waters went down and the ark was grounded on dry land on the mountain of Ararat.

But there was still a lot of water all around.

Forty days later, Noah opened up a window in the ark and released a raven and a dove. The raven flew backwards and forwards over the water and did not come back to the ark. The dove looked for a dry place to land but when it could not find one it came back to Noah in the ark.

Noah put out his hand and took the dove back into the safety of the ark.

Seven days later Noah released the dove again.
This time the bird came back in the evening with
an olive leaf in its beak.

Noah knew that the water was going down.
The trees were now visible above the surface of
the water.

A week later when the dove was released she
did not return. She could now live on the land.

Noah waited for twenty nine days and then opened the door of the ark. The flood water had disappeared. After eight more weeks the earth was dry.

'You may leave the ark now,' God told Noah. 'Take your wife, your sons and their wives with you. Let all the birds and animals and reptiles go too.'

Noah worshipped God. He built an altar and on it he sacrificed the animals that God had said were suitable. The Lord was pleased with Noah and his sacrifice.

'I will never again destroy the earth completely,' God promised, 'even when the people do terrible things.'

God made another promise. 'As long as the world exists, there will always be a planting time and a harvest time, cold and heat, summer and winter, day and night.'

Noah and his family would be able to start working on the land, growing their crops, knowing that God would not flood the earth completely again.God blessed Noah and his sons.

'You will have many children who will live all over the world. You will have power over the animals.'

God made a special promise (called a covenant) with Noah and his sons. 'Never again will I destroy all living creatures with a flood; never again will a flood destroy the whole earth.'

As a sign of the promise, God showed Noah a rainbow in the sky. Every time there is a rainbow it is a reminder of God's amazing promise to Noah and to us.

Noah found safety from God's anger by obeying God's word and going into the ark. God has provided a place of safety for us from his anger at sin, if we obey his word and trust in the Lord Jesus Christ. He is our place of safety.

When you see a rainbow, remember that all God's promises are true and faithful.